Ludwig van Beethoven

Symphony No. 8 in F major / F-Dur
Op. 93

Edited by / Herausgegeben von
Richard Clarke

EULENBURG

EAS 193
ISBN 978-3-7957-6593-4
ISMN 979-0-2002-2625-6

© 2015 Ernst Eulenburg & Co GmbH, Mainz
for Europe excluding the British Isles
Ernst Eulenburg Ltd, London
for all other countries
CD ℗ 1996 NAXOS Rights US, Inc.
CD © 2015 Ernst Eulenburg Ltd, London

Ernst Eulenburg Ltd
48 Great Marlborough Street
London W1F 7BB

Contents / Inhalt

Allegro vivace e con brio

Allegretto scherzando

Tempo di Menuetto

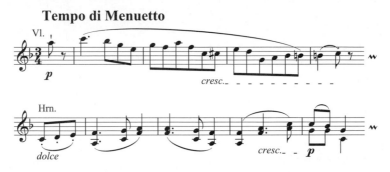

Allegro vivace

Preface

Composed: 1811/1812 in Linz
First performance: 27 February 1814 in Vienna
Original publisher: S.A.Steiner & Co., Vienna, 1816
Instrumentation: 2 Flutes, 2 Oboes, 2 Clarinets, 2 Bassoons –
2 Horns, 2 Trumpets – Timpani – Strings
Duration: ca. 25 minutes

Beethoven probably began work on his Eighth Symphony in May 1812, in other words almost immediately after completing Symphony No. 7. Work went quickly and, it would seem, relatively smoothly, and the autograph score was completed by October. The Seventh Symphony had been conceived in a great burst of restored creative energy after a rest-cure in the Bohemian spa-town of Teplitz the previous year, and it is tempting to view the Eighth Symphony as another product of that same artistic 'return to life'. The two works certainly have features in common. The Seventh Symphony is in A major, but at certain crucial stages that home tonality is dramatically challenged by the distant key of F major. In the Eighth Symphony, F major becomes the tonic, with A major now experienced as challenger: obliquely in the remarkable transition from first to second subject in the *Allegro vivace e con brio* (I, bars 34–36), unambiguously at bb136–143, and still more emphatically in the finale (bb151–157). The restoration of the tonic in the latter case (bb157ff.) is achieved by the delicious use of bassoon and timpani in octaves, *pianissimo*, one of the most frequently admired passages in this Symphony. The anapaestic rhythm in the second movement's theme (violins, bb1–2) similarly echoes the Seventh Symphony's recurring use of this propulsive rhythmic pattern, though as with the tonal contrasts outlined above, in the Eighth Symphony the manner is more relaxed, less obsessive.

On first inspection, the Eighth Symphony may seem relatively slight. It is the shortest of all Beethoven's symphonies, and while its neighbours, the Seventh and Ninth, take dramatic risks with classical formal conventions, the middle two movements of the Eighth look back affectionately to the spirit and techniques of Beethoven's teacher Joseph Haydn. There is no lyrical or dramatic probing of depths in the second movement (it is hardly a 'slow' movement at all), and the third is no muscular Beethovenian scherzo, rather a charmingly old-fashioned minuet. But appearances are deceptive. Beethoven's irrepressibly adventurous spirit can be seen at work throughout the score. The first movement's abrupt transition (bb30–38) mentioned above is a potent example, as is the exhilarating dissonant build-up to the return of the first theme in b190, given the extreme (and for Beethoven highly unusual) marking of *fff*. The *fff* marking returns for the climactic German Sixth chord in the coda (b349), only to fade rapidly for the deft *pianissimo* return of the movement's opening phrase in the last two bars. The contrasts are extreme; it is only the scale that is reduced.

For the best part of two centuries, the *Allegretto scherzando* was believed to have been inspired by the recent invention of the metronome by Johann Nepomuk Mälzel, for whose mechanical orchestra, the Panharmonicon, Beethoven composed his *Battle Symphony* in 1813. According to tradition, the second movement's theme was derived from a humorous canon Beethoven wrote mocking Mälzel's device, to the words 'Ta-ta-ta-ta... lieber Maelzel'. However pleasing it might be to think that the movement's rapid growling *fortissimo* string figures represent Beethoven's mounting fury at the robotic metronome-like chugging of the repeated wood-wind chords, both the story and the canon turn out to be an invention of a different kind by Beethoven's far-from-reliable biographer Anton Schindler.[1] The humour is real enough how-ever, and one can also sense Beethoven's delight in paradox in following a not-quite 'slow' movement marked 'scherzando' with, instead of the expected scherzo, a stately 'Tempo di Menuetto' which, in Barry Cooper's words, 'seems to mock 18th-century convention'.[2] The trio, on the other hand, with its bucolic horns and clarinets and comically labouring 'soli' cello accompaniment, is clearly a parody of the *Ländler*, the minuet's Austrian country cousin, with its characteristic heavy down beat.

As for the finale, its form is so novel that even some of the most eminent commentators have been unable to agree as to how to categorize it. For Lewis Lockwood, the form is 'more or less that of a sonata form but with two codas'.[3] For Tovey there is only one coda, but it is 'a coda [tail] that is nearly as long as the whole body of the movement'.[4] For Robert Simpson the finale 'is at once a simple rondo and a very elaborate true sonata movement; there are two developments and two recapitulations'.[5] What Tovey calls the 'coda', Lockwood the 'first coda' and Simpson the 'second development' begins at b267. After that it is up to the listener to decide how to make sense of this remarkable structure, but clearly the climactic point comes after the intrusive unison C sharp that disturbs the first theme (b17) has been rationalized as the dominant of F *sharp* minor (b379) and then jerked back violently into F major in bb391–392. Having re-established F major for good, in the closing moments Beethoven revels in the pure sound of the tonic major third (bb450–469), *sforzando* at first, then passed around the wind sections *pianissimo*. It forms a fittingly fantastical conclusion to a symphony whose 'ingenuity, subtle humour, and extraordinary originality' are 'easily masked by its superficially conventional appearance'.[6]

Stephen Johnson

[1] Lewis Lockwood, *Beethoven: The Music and the Life* (New York, 2003), 234–5
[2] Barry Cooper, Introduction to *Beethoven: Symphony No.8* (Bärenreiter Urtext edn., Kassel, 1999), iv
[3] Lockwood, op. cit., 236
[4] Donald Francis Tovey, *Essays in Musical Analysis*, Vol.I (London, 1935), 67
[5] Robert Simpson, *Beethoven Symphonies* (London, 1970), 52
[6] Cooper, op. cit., v

Vorwort

komponiert: 1811/1812 in Linz
Uraufführung: 27. Februar 1814 in Wien
Originalverlag: S. A. Steiner & Co., Wien, 1816
Orchesterbesetzung: 2 Flöten, 2 Oboen, 2 Klarinetten, 2 Fagotte –
2 Hörner, 2 Trompeten – Pauken – Streicher
Spieldauer: etwa 25 Minuten

Beethoven begann mit der Arbeit an seiner 8. Sinfonie vermutlich im Mai 1812, mit anderen Worten fast unmittelbar nach der Fertigstellung seiner 7. Sinfonie. Er kam mit der Arbeit schnell und, wie es scheint, relativ reibungslos voran, so dass die autographe Partitur im Oktober vollendet wurde. Die 7. Sinfonie war in einem großen Ausbruch von wiederhergestellter kreativer Energie nach einer Erholungskur in der böhmischen Bäderstadt Teplitz im vorangegangenen Jahr konzipiert worden. So ist es verlockend, die 8. Sinfonie als ein weiteres Ergebnis dieser künstlerischen „Rückkehr ins Leben" einzustufen. Die beiden Werke haben sicherlich gemeinsame Merkmale. Die 7. Sinfonie steht in A-Dur, aber in den entscheidenden Momenten wird diese Grundtonart durch die entfernte Tonart F-Dur dramatisch infrage gestellt. In der 8. Sinfonie bildet F-Dur die Tonika, nun mit A-Dur als Kontrast: indirekt in der bemerkenswerten Überleitung vom ersten zum zweiten Thema im Allegro vivace e con brio (I, T. 34–36), eindeutig in den Takten 136 bis 143 und noch nachdrücklicher im Finale (T. 151–157). Die Wiederherstellung der Tonika im letzteren Fall (T. 157ff.) wird durch die wunderbare Verwendung von Fagott und Pauken in Oktaven – im Pianissimo – erreicht; es handelt sich um eine der beeindruckendsten Passagen dieser Sinfonie. Der anapästische Rhythmus im Thema des zweiten Satzes (Violinen, T. 1–2) erinnert an die wiederholte Verwendung dieses fesselnden rhythmischen Modells in der 7. Sinfonie, allerdings durch die oben beschriebenen tonartlichen Gegensätze lockerer und weniger zwanghaft.

Die 8. Sinfonie mag auf den ersten Blick relativ einfach erscheinen. Es handelt sich um die kürzeste aller Beethoven-Sinfonien, und während die beiden benachbarten Sinfonien, die 7. und die 9. Sinfonie, formal dramatische Risiken hinsichtlich der klassischen Konventionen eingehen, blicken die beiden mittleren Sätze der 8. Sinfonie liebevoll zurück zum Geist und zu den Techniken von Beethovens Lehrer Joseph Haydn. Man findet im zweiten Satz kein lyrisches oder dramatisches Ausprobieren von Tiefgründigkeit (es ist eigentlich kaum ein „langsamer" Satz), und der dritte Satz ist kein kraftvolles beethovensches Scherzo, sondern eher ein reizendes, traditionelles Menuett. Aber der Schein trügt. Beethovens unerschütterlicher risikofreudiger Geist lässt sich in der Partitur des gesamten Werkes erkennen. Die oben erwähnte plötzliche Überleitung im ersten Satz (T. 30–38) ist hierfür ein aussagekräftiges Beispiel, genauso wie die spannende dissonante Vorbereitung auf die Wiederkehr des ersten Themas in T. 190 mit der extremen (und für Beethoven höchst unüblichen) Dynamik *fff*. Das Forte-Fortissimo kehrt in der Coda für den Höhepunkt auf dem Dominantnonakkord (T. 349) wieder, um sogleich für die sichere Rückkehr der Anfangsphrase des Satzes in den letzten beiden Takten wieder auszuklingen. Die Gegensätze sind extrem, nur die Tonleiter ist verkürzt.

Fast zwei Jahrhunderte lang glaubte man, dass das Allegretto scherzando von der damaligen Erfindung des Metronoms durch Johann Nepomuk Mälzel inspiriert gewesen sei, für dessen mechanisches Orchester, das Panharmonikon, Beethoven 1813 seine Schlachtensinfonie *Wellingtons Sieg oder die Schlacht bei Vittoria* komponiert hatte. Der Überlieferung nach wurde das Thema des zweiten Satzes von einem heiteren Kanon abgeleitet, den Beethoven schrieb, um Mälzels Instrument zu den Worten „Ta ta ta ta ... lieber Mälzel" nachzuahmen. Auch wenn es einem gefallen könnte, die in diesem Satz schnell brummenden Streicherfiguren im Fortissimo als Beethovens wachsende Wut gegenüber dem roboterhaften metronomartigen Tuckern der sich wiederholenden Holzbläserakkorde darzustellen, hat sich herausgestellt, dass sowohl diese Geschichte als auch der Kanon selbst Erfindungen des wenig glaubwürdigen Beethoven-Biographen Anton Schindler sind.[1] Der Humor ist trotzdem deutlich erkennbar, und man kann Beethovens Freude am Paradoxen wahrnehmen, wenn auf einen nicht gerade „langsamen", als „Scherzando" bezeichneten Satz, statt des erwarteten Scherzos ein getragenes „Tempo di Menuetto" folgt, das laut Barry Cooper „ein wenig die Gepflogenheiten des 18. Jahrhunderts zu parodieren scheint."[2] Das Trio hingegen mit seinen ländlich klingenden Hörnern und Klarinetten und der lustigen Solo-Cello-Begleitung ist eindeutig eine Parodie auf den Ländler, dem volkstümlichen österreichischen Pendant des Menuetts, mit der charakteristisch schweren ersten Zählzeit.

Was das Finale betrifft, so ist seine Form so neuartig, dass selbst die bedeutendsten Kritiker es nicht übereinstimmend einordnen konnten. Für Lewis Lockwood steht der Satz „in einer mehr oder weniger strengen Sonatenform mit allerdings zwei Codas."[3] Für Tovey gibt es nur eine Coda, aber es sei „eine Coda, die beinahe so lang wie der ganze Satz ist."[4] Für Robert Simpson ist das Finale „gleichzeitig ein einfaches Rondo und ein sehr raffinierter echter Sonatensatz; es gibt zwei Durchführungen und zwei Reprisen."[5] Was Tovey als „die Coda", Lockwood als „die erste Coda" und Simpson als „die zweite Durchführung" bezeichnet, beginnt in Takt 267. Danach bleibt dem Zuhörer die Entscheidung überlassen, wie diese bemerkenswerte Struktur einen Sinn ergeben kann. Doch der Höhepunkt erfolgt eindeutig, nachdem das aufdringliche Unisono in Cis, welches das erste Thema (T. 17) stört, durch die Dominante in fis-Moll aufgelöst (T. 379) und dann in den Takten 391 bis 392 kraftvoll in F-Dur zurückgeführt wird. Nachdem die Tonart F-Dur wiederhergestellt ist, schwärmt Beethoven im reinen Tonika-Dur-Dreiklang (T. 450–469), zuerst im Sforzando, dann pianissimo in den Bläserstimmen. Dies

---

[1] Vgl. Lewis Lockwood: *Beethoven. Seine Musik. Sein Leben* (Kassel, 2009), S. 183.
[2] Barry Cooper: Einleitung zu *Beethoven: Symphonie Nr. 8 in F-Dur* (Kassel, 1999), S. IX.
[3] Lockwood, a. a. O., S. 183.
[4] Donald Francis Tovey: *Essays in Musical Analysis*, Bd. 1 (London, 1935), S. 67.
[5] Robert Simpson: *Beethoven's Symphonies* (London, 1970), S. 52.

bildet einen ausgesprochen passenden Schluss einer Sinfonie, die „reich an Einfällen, feinem Humor und außergewöhnlicher Originalität" ist, „was leicht durch ihren etwas konventionellen äußeren Habitus verdeckt wird."[6]

Stephen Johnson
Übersetzung: Uta Pastowski

---

[6] Cooper, a. a. O., S. X.

Symphony No. 8

Ludwig van Beethoven
(1770–1827)

Op. 93

I. **Allegro vivace e con brio** (♩. = 69)

EAS 193

Edited by Richard Clarke
© 2015 Ernst Eulenburg Ltd, London
and Ernst Eulenburg & Co GmbH, Mainz

4

69
B
Fl. 1 2
Ob. 1 2
Cl. (B♭) 1 2
Fg. 1 2
Cor. (F) 1 2
Tr. (F) 1 2
Timp.
Vl. I II
Vla.
Vc. Cb.
a 2
1.
p dolce
p
76
ff
Vc.
Cb.

EAS 193

14

ritard.　　a tempo

ritard.
a tempo
246
Fl. 1
Ob. 1 2
Cl. (B♭) 1 2
Fg. 1 2
Cor. (F) 1 2
Timp.
Vl. I II
Vla.
Vc. Cb.
1.
(pizz.)
arco
pp
253
Fl. 1 2
Tr. (F) 1 2
cresc.
sf

II. Allegretto scherzando (♪ = 88)

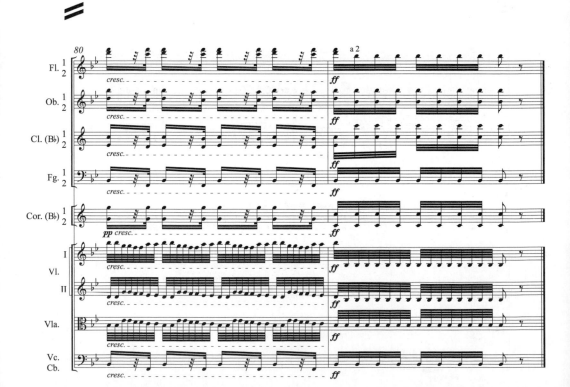

III. Tempo di Menuetto (♩ = 126)

Menuetto da capo al Fine

IV. Allegro vivace (♩ = 84)

17
Fl. 1 2
Ob. 1 2
Cl. (B♭) 1 2
Fg. 1 2
Cor. (F) 1 2
Tr. (F) 1 2
Timp.
Vl. I II
Vla.
Vc.
Cb.
ff
sempre ff
1.
23
Vc. Cb.
a 2

82
Fl. 1 2
Ob. 1 2
Cl. (B♭) 1 2
Fg. 1 2
Cor. (F) 1 2
Tr. (F) 1 2
Timp.
Vl. I II
Vla.
Vc. Cb.
più f
88
B
ff
p

58

66

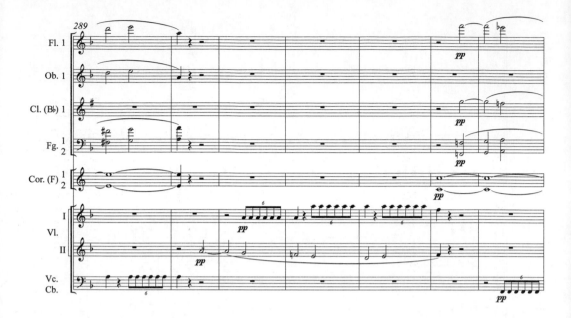

68